# Write

*for your*

# Soul

Oh, the worst of all tragedies

is not to die young,

but to live

until I am seventy-five

and yet not ever

to have truly lived.

THE REV. DR. MARTIN LUTHER KING, JR.

# *Write*
### *for your*
# *Soul*

## The Whys and Hows of Journaling

*by Jeff and Mindy Caliguire*

Soul Care™

For information: Soul Care Communications, LLC, PMB 134, 25 East Hoyle St., Norwood, MA 02062
e-mail: writeback@soulcare.com

Printed in the United States of America
ISBN 1-929794-14-2

*Dedicated to*
*the author and perfecter of our faith*
*and those who share the journey.*

# Contents

In my travels,
I find that most people today
are restless and hungry
to get "into the game"
and experience the deeper meaning
of their lives.

They just don't know where to start.

KEN BLANCHARD, CO-AUTHOR,
*THE ONE MINUTE MANAGER*

# What About Your Soul?

*"Do you think it's dead?"*
*"I don't know."*
*"Maybe we can get it to come back."*
*"No, let's just get rid of it. It's not like it's very pretty."*

*What do you do with a barren, shriveled Ficus tree?,* we
wondered as newlyweds ten years ago. Once an impres-
sive and lush tropical tree given to us as a gift, it had
been reduced to bare branches and dry soil. Filling a
quarter of our living room, it had been an oasis of life in
our dark apartment. Yet, as our lives became busier and
more complicated, we neglected it. Living on minimal
water, little sunlight and the trauma of being knocked
over a few times by a carelessly pushed vacuum, its life
slowly began to ebb, then vanish.

I want to live my life,
not have life live me.

LORI PETERSON, FRIEND

In the same inadvertent way, many of us overlook the care of our own souls.  As urgencies and emergencies multiply and we get knocked about by careless intruders, attention to our inner life can wane.  No, not intentionally, but it diminishes nonetheless.  Recognizing the danger of this condition, Jesus warned, "What does it profit a man if he gains the whole world, yet loses his soul?"  Our souls have great value, and should not get lost along the way.  As you care for the outer you, care for the inner you, too.  We are designed with souls meant to flourish like healthy trees.

But how do you care for your soul?  Many products inform our minds, bring fitness and health to our bodies and entertain us, but few help us care for our souls.

## OUR STORY

Neither of us set out to neglect the care of our souls.  We both sought understanding through rigorous academic training; we even studied at seminary.  We read books and agreed with authors that taught "private victory pre-

Those who
cannot remember the past
are condemned
to repeat it.

GEORGE SANTAYANA, SPANISH PHILOSOPHER,
*THE LIFE OF REASON*

cedes public victory" (Covey) and "the life which is unexamined is not worth living." (Socrates). But when our lives turned unstable and even stormy, we struggled. *Is life supposed to feel like this?,* we questioned. *Is real change possible?* The persistent ache caused us to wonder if our souls had become like that Ficus, barren from benign neglect.

Over the last few years, through that season of pain, we learned what we had overlooked: the care of our souls. We discovered things which restored vitality including music, reading, building friendships, enjoying nature, solitude, prayer, and tuning in to the lessons of our lives through journaling.

As we journal we pray to God, we ask ourselves probing questions, we think through issues, we put on paper the "stuff" tumbling about in our heads. We become more connected with God and ourselves, and, ultimately, with others.

*What does that look like?*

## THE REAL STUFF OF
## JEFF AND MINDY'S JOURNALS

*"Once again, I showed up late after promising to be home for dinner. Why do I keep doing this? I really do want to be home. Somehow I believe that if I don't finish my 'to-do's,' I'm a failure! When I walked in, she expressed her disappointment and I got all defensive. When I finally just apologized and admitted I blew it, things cooled off. Will I ever learn?"*

*(Jeff's journal)*

*"'How do you feel?' 'What do you need right now?' How should I know? If I knew that, I probably wouldn't be in such a bad space. Kari's questions are just sincere attempts to help. I hadn't a clue how to answer her. Do I need some time away, some time for myself? I'm feeling a bit numb right now. That can't be good."*

*(Mindy's journal)*

*"Um ... Mommy?... Mommy?"...*
*"What Jonathan?," I said impatiently from the front seat*
*of the van.*
*"Um, Mommy?  I love you Mommy."*
*"Oh, thank you Jonathan" I said.  "I love you too, Honey."*
*(pause) "Um ... Daddy? ... Daddy?"*
*"What Jonathan?" (very expectantly)*
*"Um ... Daddy, could you please turn the light off?"*
*We could not stop laughing.*

> *(Car conversation recorded in Mindy's journal)*

That's the real stuff of our lives. The journal acts as a window into the soul.  In it, we chronicle, draw out and reflect the real us.

## CAN ANYONE LEARN TO JOURNAL?

If you think journaling is a great practice for reclusive ascetics but couldn't work for you, we hope to change your mind.

The soul,
though at all times hidden,
is at all times revealed, expressing itself
through everything we say and do.

Through the ordinary brushstrokes
of everyday life,
a portrait of our soul is being painted.

KEN GIRE,
*WINDOWS OF THE SOUL*

For me (extroverted Jeff), I could never have imagined leaving sleep, people or noise to do anything by myself ... especially involving a pen and a journal! But now I dislike completing a day without some time to write in my journal. For the last four years, I've been consistently rising around 5:30 AM without even setting my alarm (even on days off!) to get in a good hour of journaling and reflection before I start my day. (Night owls, please don't try this at home, at least not right away! Being an early bird is not a prerequisite for journaling.)

For me (more inhibited Mindy), I didn't mind being alone; I just thought I had nothing to say. Why write what is obvious? It doesn't change anything. But I've found that my journal opens me to change, and that, in turn, can transform many aspects of my life. I've come to depend on the observations I make of myself and my life.

How better to keep in touch
with God's work in me
than to record
what is happening to me
day after day?

HENRI J.M. NOUWEN,
*THE ROAD TO DAYBREAK*

# Why Journal?

Journals give us a place in which to record our insights into the ordinary and extraordinary occurrences of everyday life. Reflections after time away, time spent with children, thoughts on new responsibilities at work ... the feeling of experiencing an earthquake, reflections on the birth of your child ... If you're open, there's a lot of life out there to learn from and remember.

Our journal helps us to see more clearly what's really going on. It acts as an "album" of thoughts and experiences. Great times, maddening events, even daily routines are imprinted on our souls whether we realize it or not. Our memories begin to serve our own growth. By consciously recording our history, the past becomes more "user-friendly" to us and more accessible to future generations.

During a time of career uncertainty, I (Jeff) piled my old journals into my car and headed off to do a study on my past. I was amazed by how much I had forgotten that actually became useful in making an important decision.

## DEVELOP YOUR "BEING" SIDE

It's just too easy to fall into the pattern of becoming "human doings" instead of human beings. The habit of journaling helps us slow down and enjoy the "being" side of life. It's relaxing. It provides a sense of planned "margin" in our full days. Journaling is also one of the few practices that helps us simplify and view what *is*, instead of what isn't. When we journal we take stock of the present.

I (Mindy) tend to be a bit compulsive about getting everything done in a day. I am a stickler with lists, planners and neatness in my life and home. Yet, in my frenzy to get everything done, I can end up missing life along the way. I definitely needed something that helped me to see the preciousness of the present. Journaling helps restore the joy.

The emotional depletion
that results from living
in crisis mode
eventually produces
a shrinking heart.

BILL AND LYNNE HYBELS,
*FIT TO BE TIED*

Hurry is
not just a
disordered
schedule.
Hurry is a
disordered
heart.

JOHN ORTBERG,
*THE LIFE YOU'VE ALWAYS WANTED*

The serenity of journal time is life-giving. And even when things get crazy, it's always good to know that you're no more than a day or so away from being able to evaluate, reflect and be still.

## EXPLORE YOUR TRUE SELF

Who am I? Why do I do the things I do? What aspects of my past affect my present? Tough questions, right? But, do you know the answers? Our more intense emotions can provide clues to our inner selves if we're willing to look and see. Intense feelings of joy, life, deep sadness or toxic anger can give us clues to the true condition of our souls.

I (Jeff) had no clue that my angry outbursts under pressure were actually coming out of a deep rooted belief that I needed to perform flawlessly in order to prove my value.

I (Mindy) had a hard time seeing how subtly destructive a "discerning spirit" can be when it is harsh and critical toward myself and others.

Journaling allows me
an objective audience
for pouring out my heart.
An inviting blank page
doesn't judge my ideas,
fears, or questions.

JULIE STAUB, FRIEND

We've been affected by our origins. But we're now responsible for what we do with what we've been given. Our "stuff," the light and the shadow, affects others. The big question is, *How are we affecting those around us?* The truth can be hard to hear.

I (Jeff) was baffled when a woman I worked closely with shared that my actions were "controlling" to her and other co-workers. *Who me?,* I inwardly protested (outwardly too, come to think of it!). Yet, with time and more pain and damage, I've discovered she was right.

Journaling becomes like a regular session with a counselor. Of course we still need others, but the journal acts as a safe place to observe, understand and then move toward change. You can't change what you don't perceive. But it doesn't make it easy. Exposing the inner journey can be difficult and dangerous at times. It's far easier to deal with the external world. But as we recognize our personality quirks, our baggage and our character flaws, change becomes possible.

## EXPOSE YOUR ANXIETY

We all express anxiety in different ways. For some, it is through nervous behavior, such as obsessive cleaning or nailbiting. For others, it is manifested through self-assailing inner conversations or external negativity. What do you do with your anxiety?

I (Mindy), prided myself in keeping a calm and cool exterior in almost any circumstance. Under pressure I presented a stoic front, while inside I carried on anguish-filled dialogues with myself and others. The problem was that over time the negative emotions (I really did have some!) in my head failed to come out of my mouth and started affecting my physical health. During a time of challenging conflicts and financial insecurity that coincided with my second pregnancy, my situation boiled over. Frightening neurological symptoms that showed no response to medication led me into a deep depression. My neurologist referred me to a counselor. His core advice: "You've got to let what's going on in your head come out of your mouth."

He was right. Life's challenges affect us. The car's transmission goes, the big presentation is tomorrow, the bank account is depleted, the doctor's report awaits us, the in-laws are coming for the weekend. How will we handle those challenges? Will we be proactive or reactive? Will we be faith-filled or fearful? By recording the struggle on paper, we at least gain the potential to make a wise decision. Exposing anxiety can be the all-important first step.

And this simple concept,

of making sure

that our daily activities

reflect our deepest core values,

is the concept that has made

all the difference

in my own life.

HYRUM SMITH,
*TEN NATURAL LAWS OF SUCCESSFUL TIME
AND LIFE MANAGEMENT*

# How to Journal

*How do I start? What do I write?*

### CREATE A LIFE HABIT

Like anything else you do to take care of your self, this requires some planning and effort. No one will make you do it or do it for you. It's been said that if you do something faithfully for 30 days in a row, it will likely become a life habit. That's what happened for us. Remember that the goal is not perfection or performance but to have your journal serve you. We write virtually every day. Others we know write more sporadically. But the main point is to write. Learn. Grow.

I (Jeff) am a well-practiced procrastinator, expert at finding shortcuts to get around long writing assignments

Whenever you find
tears in your eyes,
especially unexpected tears,
it is well to pay
the closest attention.

FREDERICK BUECHNER,
*WHISTLING IN THE DARK*

and daily routines. Our lawn got so overgrown last year that our kids began losing toys (even buckets and bikes!) out there.

The key is to start slowly and write a little each day. If you don't have much to say, that's fine. There will be days when you'll more than make up for it. Both of us love to begin our days with a journal time. For us, it's the best way to start a productive, positive day.

Another part of creating a life habit of journaling is to find a comfortable place.

I (Jeff) like going to a nearby lake to write in my journal whenever I can. When it's cold, I sit in the car with the heater on. When it's warm, I sit at the water's edge.

The problem is not entirely
in finding the room of one's own,
the time alone, difficult as that is.

The problem is more
how to still the soul
in the midst of its activities.

ANNE MORROW LINDBERGH,
*GIFT FROM THE SEA*

For me (Mindy), the best spot is a coffee shop in the center of town. The noise doesn't bother me and even helps keep me awake during the early hours! Our living room couch is always a great option, as long as I get there before our precious little ones wake up. And both of us agree that a steaming cup of coffee goes great with a journal. Discover what works for you, and keep at it.

## STRUCTURE WHAT WORKS FOR YOU

What do you write? Though many of us don't like to over-structure our journals, it can be helpful to work with a format. It's even helpful to have some easy starters to prompt spontaneity, particularly if you're new to journaling.

Each of our journal entries starts with the day, the date, and the place we're writing from (i.e. home, the lake, coffee shop). Some entries flow for pages from that point. Others stop after a few lines or paragraphs.

Do not try to be someone
you are not.
It will cause you great stress
and deep frustration.

BOBB BIEHL,
*STOP SETTING GOALS*

Some ideas...

- ❖ *Look back ("Yesterday I...")*

- ❖ *Record your dreams (Particularly recurring, troubling or exciting dreams. If you're bold, try to analyze them. You may want to find a book on the topic.)*

- ❖ *Fun moments (Your birdie on the 18th hole!)*

- ❖ *Pray on paper ("Dear God...")*

- ❖ *What you're learning lately (insights, wisdom, mistakes)*

- ❖ *Work through decisions (write out pros and cons)*

- ❖ *Quotes or stories you want to remember (something you read or that a friend told you)*

- ❖ *Observations about how life works ("Malls instill a need for more. When I go there, I feel dissatisfied with what I have.")*

A diary
helps build up the muscles
of your personality...
In truth,
those of us who keep diaries
cannot stop.

ALEXANDRA STODDARD,
*LIVING A BEAUTIFUL LIFE*

- ❖ *Precious moments (what your 3-year-old said to his baby brother)*

- ❖ *Scenes you want to keep with you (the incredible sunset over Lake Pleasant)*

- ❖ *Ideas or goals for the future ("Go whitewater rafting this summer.")*

- ❖ *Your values*

- ❖ *Mission statements (personal or family)*

- ❖ *Notes from sermons or lectures*

## QUESTION YOURSELF

Problems exist. Often we don't have answers because we haven't asked the right questions. Questions help us see potential solutions that lie just below the surface. We have a consultant friend whose advice is in considerable demand simply because he is committed to discovering and posing profound questions. He deftly brainstorms the right questions that uncover creative new solutions.

The journal is a safe place in which to pose your own great questions, then seek answers.

Here are a few questions from our journals...

- ❖ *Why do I keep doing this?*

- ❖ *What do I need?*

- ❖ *What's my next step?*

- ❖ *Why do I feel so numb? out of control? hurt? angry? selfish?*

- ❖ *How do my actions reveal what I truly believe?*

- ❖ *How can I express my love to her?*

- ❖ *How can I help him without trying to fix him?*

- ❖ *Why am I getting so involved in this?*

- ❖ *What am I afraid of?*

- ❖ *What's the worst that can happen?*

You have two choices;

you can either accept it

and make the best of it,

or make yourself and

everyone around you

miserable.

MINDY'S NEUROLOGIST

Suffering
always changes us,
but it does not
necessarily change us
for the better.

JOHN ORTBERG,
*THE LIFE YOU'VE ALWAYS WANTED*

## DRAW

While artistic people may find value in sketching their ideas, I (Jeff) can't draw much more than stick figures. But I do find it useful to make a visual representation of my emotional status.

I start in the center of a blank page by writing the dominant emotion I'm experiencing. (Often it's anxiety.) Then I reflect upon my circumstances to discover what contributed to this feeling. I'm usually surprised by how much is involved. Next, I draw two lines downward depicting my options at this point. One is usually to do nothing. The other invites me to consider how I can respond with faith in a sovereign God who "works all things together for the good." (Romans 8:28).

I found that though I believe in God, my day to day struggles suggest that I don't. Under each of the "do nothing" or "trust God" options, I list what I envision the outcomes would be for myself and others.

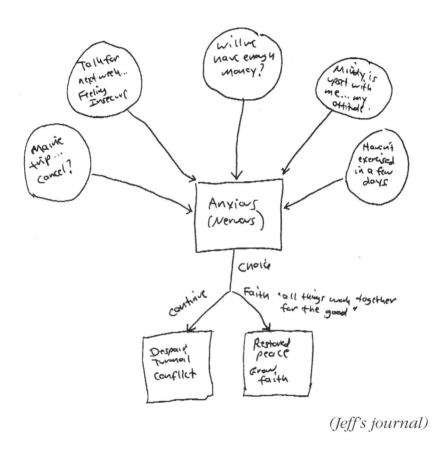

*(Jeff's journal)*

As I do this, I gain a greater sense of my freedom to choose my response to these circumstances, and my faith grows.

My dominant emotion this day (referring to the journal drawing at left) was being anxious/nervous. After reflection, I realized several factors contributed to this (shown by the circles which join to the central box). My options, I recognized, were to do nothing, to continue, with the likely outcomes of discouragement and depression, or to trust in God's "future grace", in which case I would likely experience rest and peace and the ability to be proactive. At that point, my next steps out of my nervous state became more clear and hopeful.

## SPEAK WITH GOD

The journal is a great way to grow spiritually. Both of us see our journals as places in which to engage in ongoing discussions with God.

Though I believe in the power of prayer, I (Jeff) used to feel guilty that my prayers were kind of disorganized, often repetitive and dull. Frequently, while praying, my active mind moved to thinking about my day's activities or a problem to be solved, and before I knew it I was off on a tangent. If I was tired, I would sometimes drift off to sleep in the middle of prayer time. I sometimes wonder how God felt when I dozed off during our conversations.

Journaling has revolutionized both of our prayer lives. It's been incredibly helpful in building an authentic relationship with God.

My (Mindy) journal almost invariably begins with, "Hi, Lord ..." Then I just write God a letter. No postage necessary and the server always works! I used to censor what I wrote to make it what I thought one ought to say to God. Lately, I'm learning to be more raw, more exposed, more honest. He knows my junk and so do I, and we move from there.

All happenings,
great and small, are parables
whereby God speaks,
the art of life
is to get the message.

MALCOLM MUGGERIDGE,
BRITISH JOURNALIST

If the God of the Universe
tells you something,
you should write it down!

HENRY BLACKABY,
*EXPERIENCING GOD*

In structuring your own prayer, you may want to enlist a format, such as the easily remembered "A.C.T.S." That stands for Adoration (expressing words of honor to God), Confession (admitting your wrongdoing), Thanksgiving (listing what you are grateful for), and Supplication (appealing to God for help in your and others' situations). Start with words of adoration and move on through each category.

The journal is also a great barometer of our hearts. Coming to God regularly and in a personal way is a reality check on what is most important. We can listen and hear God's voice. The Psalmist wrote, "Be still and know that I am God" (Psalm 46:10). As we slow down to hear God's voice, we record His messages for application.

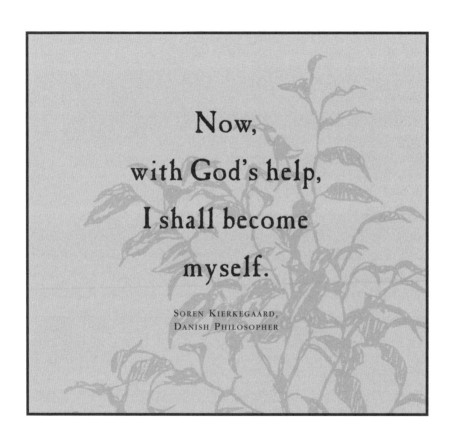

Now,

with God's help,

I shall become

myself.

Soren Kierkegaard,
Danish Philosopher

# The Value of a Journal You Can Keep

As you might imagine, when you record your life's journey on paper, that paper becomes extremely valuable. The journal holds a part of you. It's worth the investment in a quality journal that is safely stored and treasured.

The true value of my journal was made clear to me (Jeff) when I lost mine on a mountain road a few years ago. I had left it on top of the car and then driven down a winding road. When I discovered it was missing, I searched that road and through the woods for more than two hours before I found it. I even enlisted the help of my mother-in-law, who graciously entered the mosquito-infested woods to join me in the search.

Store your journals in a safe place (not on top of a car!). Date them (or label them by topic) on the cover or the

Once you find
a type of notebook
you feel comfortable with,
stock up on them—
choosing the right journal
just for you
is the important first step.

ALEXANDRA STODDARD,
*LIVING A BEAUTIFUL LIFE*

binding for easy reference, then file them on your bookshelf. We now regret that we used poor quality spiral notebooks in the past and misplaced them in attic boxes and piles. Going back to them for referral becomes almost impossible this way. Invest in high quality, well bound journals that will last you a lifetime. Even if you're the only one who reads them (you may feel safer that way), you'll treasure your journals for years to come.

Don't let your soul become like our Ficus tree! Pay attention to it. Feed it and nurture it. Record and reflect. Write for your soul. Your life will be richer because you did.

JEFF AND MINDY CALIGUIRE
NORWOOD, MASSACHUSETTS

## THE AUTHORS

Since their college sweetheart days at Cornell University, Jeff and Mindy Caliguire have engaged in a quest to nurture their souls and create forums to help others do the same. After graduating from Dallas Theological Seminary, working in corporate America and interning at Willow Creek Community Church in Chicago, they founded Operation Beacon Street Inc., Beacon Community Church and Boston Sports Fellowship in the Boston area. Jeff is also the author of "Life in Jesus" and co-author of "Real Connection: Discovering the Spiritual Life."

Jeff and Mindy attribute the education of their souls to the input of challenging mentors, insightful literature, over ten years of journaling, and God's "severe mercy" of pain. They reside in Norwood, Massachusetts, with their three children, Jeffrey, Jonathan and Joshua ("The J Team!").